FALL GUYS:
Beginner's Guide

CHERRY LAKE PUBLISHING • ANN ARBOR, MICHIGAN

by Josh Gregory

CHERRY LAKE PRESS

Published in the United States of America by Cherry Lake Publishing
Ann Arbor, Michigan
www.cherrylakepublishing.com

Reading Adviser: Beth Walker Gambro, MS, Ed., Reading Consultant, Yorkville, IL

Cherry Lake Press is an imprint of Cherry Lake Publishing Group

Library of Congress Cataloging-in-Publication Data has been filed and is available
at catalog.loc.gov

Cherry Lake Publishing Group would like to acknowledge the work of the Part-
nership for 21st Century Learning, a Network of Battelle for Kids. Please visit
http://www.batelleforkids.org/networks/p21 for more information.

Printed in the United States of America
Corporate Graphics

Contents

Chapter 1

A Surprising Smash

On August 4, 2020, the release of *Fall Guys: Ultimate Knockout* took video game fans by surprise. Within just one day of its release, the game attracted more than 1.5 million players from all

Fall Guys is one of the brightest and most colorful video games available today.

In the early days of *Fall Guys*, players would often get stuck waiting a long time for their games to start, if they started at all.

around the world. It was so popular that its **servers** couldn't handle the demand. Far more players than expected were logging on at the same time and trying to join matches. This led to all kinds of technical issues with the game. For several days, players had trouble starting new matches. Other times, matches would suddenly end partway through, with the game display-ing error messages. When games have these kinds of issues, it usually draws negative attention. But in the case of *Fall Guys*, it only made more people interested in trying the game. Overnight, *Fall Guys* became the only thing many video game fans wanted to talk about.

What made *Fall Guys* such a hit? It wasn't part of a long-running series, and it was created by a little-known team of **developers**. It simply wasn't the sort of big-name, hyped game that typically sells millions of copies on launch day. However, the game's colorful art style, simple controls, and wacky sense of humor grabbed people's attention right away.

It also helped that many players were able to download the game for free during its first month. The

Want to dress up as french fries or a disco ball? No matter what you wear, you'll probably end up out of control and flying through the air at some point.

When this many characters crowd together, something funny is bound to happen sooner or later.

PlayStation 4 version of *Fall Guys* was given away to all subscribers of the PlayStation Plus service. Many players who might not have normally bought the game decided to give it a shot. Some of them were hooked right away. They started posting funny screen-shots and videos on social media, and more people started to take notice of the game. Popular streamers went live with *Fall Guys* on their channels. Word spread very quickly, and the game became a viral sensation.

This unexpected success caught the developers of *Fall Guys* off guard. The game was created by a British studio called Mediatonic. Founded in 2005, Mediatonic worked on dozens of games before making *Fall Guys*. However, almost all of these games were small projects that could be played through web browsers or mobile apps. *Fall Guys* was the team's biggest project yet. It would be competing against big-budget multiplayer smashes such as *Fortnite* and *Call of Duty*.

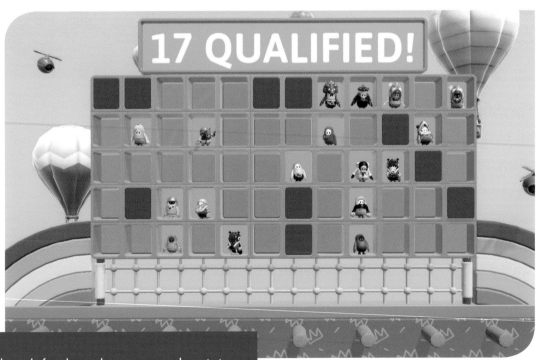

At the end of each round, you can see who gets to move on and who has been knocked out.

PUSH YOUR BALL! 7% 7% 8%

Some rounds require players to team up. Here, teams have to push a huge ball across an obstacle course.

There was no guarantee that it would be able to stand out in the crowd and gain an audience. However, the team was confident that they had a good idea on their hands.

What is *Fall Guys* all about? Each match is a series of mini-games where players have to avoid obstacles or complete simple tasks like knocking soccer balls into goals. In each round, some players are knocked out, while others get to continue on. The last player standing is the winner. The game's developers were inspired by TV game shows where people try to complete obstacle courses as quickly as possible. As a result, each match of *Fall Guys* is called a "show."

The team at Mediatonic quickly sorted out the server issues that affected the game at launch. Once they had adjusted their systems to keep up with demand, they were able to start expanding *Fall Guys* and making it even better. They had to keep players coming back and show that *Fall Guys* was more than just the flavor of the week.

In March 2021, Epic Games announced that it had purchased Mediatonic. One of the largest video game companies in the world, Epic is behind mega-hits such as *Fortnite* and *Gears of War*. This was a sign that *Fall Guys* had truly hit the big time. The game's development team had already tripled in size since launch. With the resources of a huge company like Epic behind them, they promised to keep making *Fall Guys* bigger and better. But they also promised that the core gameplay that fans know and love would not be changing. If the long-term successes of games

Looking to join in the fun of *Fall Guys*? If you have any device that plays modern video games, there's probably a way for you to play. When the game first launched in August 2020, it was only available for Windows PCs and the PlayStation 4 console. But in early 2021, the developers at Mediatonic announced that they would also **port** the game to Nintendo Switch and Xbox consoles. This would make sure as many people as possible could see what the *Fall Guys* hype was all about. If you enjoy watching your favorite streamers play the game, consider trying it yourself!

like *Fortnite* and *Rocket League* are a sign of things to come, *Fall Guys* will keep players busy for years. There's never been a better time to start playing!

Chapter 2

Battle of the Beans

Fall *Guys* is designed so new players can pick it up and start having fun right away. The controls are simple and the object of the game is always clear. You don't have much to learn if you just want to try out a couple of casual matches. But even though

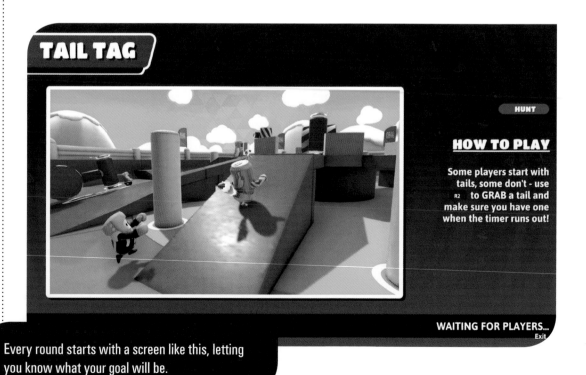

Every round starts with a screen like this, letting you know what your goal will be.

It only takes a single press of the button from the main menu to start playing a match of *Fall Guys*.

Fall Guys is a simple game at first, there is a lot more to it than you might think.

When you start up the game, you'll probably notice that the main menu is pretty simple. All you need to do to jump into a match is press the button marked "PLAY!" In just a few seconds, you will be thrown into the first round of a show. Each show begins with 60 players. During a round, between 25 percent and 50 percent of the players will be knocked out. The rest will move on to the next round.

Each round offers a slightly different challenge. For example, you might need to reach the finish line of an obstacle course. Or you might be teamed up with other players and asked to push a ball through a maze. The loading screen for each round will give you a short description of what you need to do to win. In all of these challenges, you will control a small, round character with stubby arms and legs. Because of their shape, *Fall Guys* characters are often called "beans" by fans.

Your bean only has a few different moves. You can walk or run in any direction. You can also jump, dive headfirst in different directions, or reach out and grab things. That's it. There are no complicated controls to learn. However, using the right moves at the right time isn't always as simple as it seems. *Fall Guys* does not have perfectly **precise** controls. Your character will feel slow and wobbly as it moves around. Obstacles often bounce you in different directions, and you can easily be knocked off-balance. *Fall Guys* was made this way on purpose. The developers wanted to create a game where funny, unexpected things could happen at any time. "That's really what the whole thing has been designed for, is to create this sense of **chaos**," lead designer Joe Walsh said in an interview.

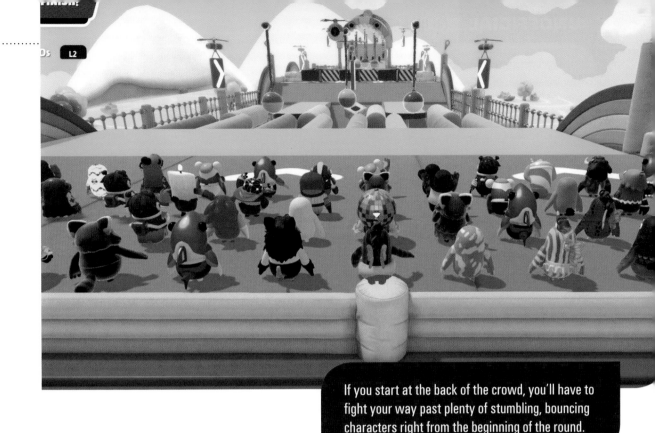

If you start at the back of the crowd, you'll have to fight your way past plenty of stumbling, bouncing characters right from the beginning of the round.

The first round of every show is always a Race event. All 60 players will be gathered at the starting line. After a short countdown, everyone will start running at once. With so many beans stuck in one area, it can be a real mess. Characters will get in your way, and you might trip and fall. On your way to the finish line, you'll have to dodge obstacles and jump across platforms. It's all about good timing and a little bit of luck. If you don't panic, you can probably make it through. The round will end once a certain number of players cross the finish line.

The next round could be another Race event. But it could also be something completely different. Each *Fall Guys* show lasts for between three and seven rounds. Aside from the first and last rounds, the goals of each round are selected at random. The first round is always a Race because the game needs to weed out some of the 60 starting players. The last round is always a special Final event. In Final events, a small group of players face off in contests where there is only one possible winner. For example, the winner

In this Final event, players compete to be the last one standing as panels of ice break and fall away one by one.

Last One Standing

Fall Guys is far from being the only popular battle royale game. This style of game blasted onto the scene in 2017 with the release of *PlayerUnknown's Battlegrounds* and *Fortnite*. Since then, all kinds of other games have tried to capture the success of those titles. There have even been battle royale versions of *Tetris* and *Super Mario*.

One thing that helps *Fall Guys* stand out from the crowd is its lighthearted tone. There is no shooting or realistic violence. The characters and environments are goofy and colorful, and the music is catchy. And of course, most players don't take the game too seriously. If you get knocked out, it's best to just laugh and start up a new match!

might be the last player to avoid falling from an ever-shrinking platform.

The other event categories are Survival, Hunt, **Logic**, and Team. Each category except for Logic has a number of different variations. At launch, there were a total of 24 different possible rounds. Since then, the developers have steadily added more to the game. Every round type in the game is designed for players to be able to figure it out the first time they play. However, if you want to win often, you'll need to learn the ins and outs of all of them.

Chapter 3

Playing in Style

At the end of each *Fall Guys* show, you'll see a screen showing your rewards. You'll get at least a little something no matter how well you did. These rewards come in the form of Fame, Crowns, and Kudos. All three are important because they let you start customizing the look of your bean. For many players, being able to change their bean's appearance

Even if you have a hard time winning in *Fall Guys*, you'll unlock plenty of costumes if you play enough.

Some of the costumes in *Fall Guys* are truly strange, and you can mix and match the pieces of all of them.

is a big part of the fun. You can dress your bean up in wacky costumes, change its color and pattern, and more. But first you'll need to build your collection of **cosmetic** items.

There are five categories of cosmetic items in *Fall Guys*. Colours are two-color combinations you can apply to your bean. Patterns change the design of these colors. For example, you might change your bean to have a zigzag pattern, or stripes. Faces are different designs for your bean's circular face area. Uppers are clothes for the upper half of your bean's body, from the head to the waist. Lowers are clothes that cover your bean from the waist down. Many Uppers and Lowers have matching sets so you can dress your bean in a complete costume. You can also mix and match them however you like. Once you have a large collection of cosmetics, the possibilities are nearly endless.

You can also unlock something called Theatrics. These are movements that your bean can perform during matches. There are two kinds: Emotes and

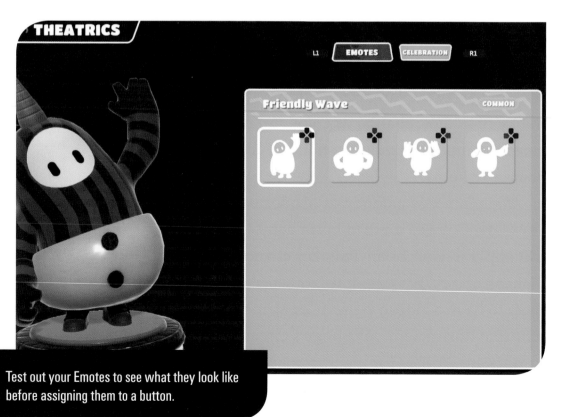

Test out your Emotes to see what they look like before assigning them to a button.

It All Adds Up

Purchasing Kudos in *Fall Guys* is a **microtransaction**. These small purchases are very popular in multiplayer video games. For just a few dollars, players can purchase a new style to show off as they play. This helps keep the game fresh over a long period of time. It also allows developers to make more money off their games.

Even though each microtransaction isn't usually very expensive, buying a lot of things can really add up over time. Keep track of how much money you are spending in *Fall Guys* and other games. You might be surprised to see the total cost after a few months of playing. And of course, always get permission from a parent before you spend money on a game.

Celebrations. Emotes can be assigned to four different buttons on your controller. When you press that button during a match, your character will perform the Emote. This could be anything from a simple wave to a brief dance move. Emotes don't give you any advantage in the game. They are just a way to show off and communicate with other players. Some players use them to **taunt** their opponents. Celebrations are a little different from Emotes. These are the movements your character will perform at the end of a match if you manage to win first place.

Finally, you can also unlock ways to customize the game's **interface**. There are two types of cosmetic items in this category: Nameplates and Nicknames. Nameplates are the rectangular boxes that show your screen name during matches. Other players will see them at various points during a match. You can unlock all kinds of different colors and patterns for them. Nicknames are funny phrases you can display on your Nameplate.

When you watch another player after you've been knocked out, you can see their Nameplate in the bottom left corner.

FALLGUYS
SEASON 4

Ends in approx. 55 Days

1 — 0/30

Earn FAME by competing in Shows!

FALLTRON DESTINY
Costume
LEGENDARY

44 45 46 47 48

5

1.21 Gigabeans

You can check out all of a season's rewards in the main menu. This way you know exactly how many levels you need to unlock the items you want.

Some cosmetics are rarer than others. Each item is labeled Uncommon, Common, Rare, Epic, or Legendary. Typically the wildest designs are in the Epic or Legendary categories. More basic options tend to have lower rarity. But don't choose your cosmetics based on their rarity level. Simply pick out the styles that look best to you. None of these options give you any advantage in the game. They are just for expressing yourself in a fun way.

So where do these cosmetic items come from? The easiest way to unlock them is to simply play the game and do your best to make it as far as you can in each match. This will earn you plenty of Fame. As you gain Fame, you will level up. Each time you raise your level, you will unlock a new item. The maximum level is 40. However, the game introduces a new set of levels and rewards with each season. Each season runs for about two months. At the end of the season, everyone is set back to level one. Any rewards you missed from the previous season are gone for good.

Along with Fame, you'll earn something called Kudos from each match you play. Kudos are a form of **currency** in *Fall Guys*. You can use them to purchase new cosmetics from an in-game store. These cosmetics are different from the ones you can unlock by leveling up. If you aren't earning Kudos as quickly as you'd like while playing, you also have the option to purchase Kudos with real money.

Crowns are the rarest form of currency in *Fall Guys*. There are only a couple of ways to get them. One is to come in first place in a match. Another is to get them as a reward for leveling up. Each season, there will be a handful of crowns available from leveling up. Like Kudos, Crowns can be used to purchase new cosmetics from the in-game store. Unlike Kudos, you cannot purchase more of them using real money. Many of the game's most desirable cosmetics require Crowns to unlock them. You'll need to win a lot of matches if you want everything that's available!

The rarest items in the in-game store often require Crowns to purchase.

Chapter 4

Winning Strategies

B y now, you probably have a good feel for *Fall Guys*. You probably also have an interesting look to set your bean apart. But it takes more than that to truly master the game. If you want to win frequently, you'll need plenty of practice. Getting to know the different types of rounds is crucial. It also

Some rounds of *Fall Guys* are more complex than others. In this one, you have to change the color of panels by walking over them while carrying a special battery.

Getting a feel for grabbing, climbing, and diving is essential to succeeding at *Fall Guys*.

helps to learn a few advanced techniques that can help you out in tricky situations.

One important thing to master early on is the game's control system. Even though you can only perform a handful of different actions, you can put them to use in interesting ways. Think about your dive move. The most basic way to use it is to get out of the way when something is about to hit you. But it has other advantages too. Try diving when you are in the middle of a jump. You should notice that it helps you

Watching the Winners

Anytime you are knocked out in a round of *Fall Guys*, you can choose to leave the game. You'll get all your rewards and you can start a new match right away. But if you decide to hang around instead, you can watch to see how the rest of the match turns out. You can flip between views of the remaining players as you follow the action. This is a great way to pick up strategies and see what you've been doing wrong. Simply watch what the best players do and try to master their moves!

travel a greater distance in the air. This is very useful when you need to get across a wide gap. If there are movable objects such as balls or blocks, you can also dive headfirst into them to knock them aside. Remember that it takes a second to get back up after you dive. Getting used to this timing will help you learn when to dive and when not to dive.

Your grab technique also has several uses. Some are obvious, such as when the game specifically tells you to pick up and carry various objects. But you can actually grab all kinds of things, even when it isn't a required part of the round. Want to jump onto a ledge that's a little too high? Jump up, then hold down the grab button at the peak of your jump. You will grab the ledge and pull yourself up!

You can also grab other players. Simply run up next to them and hold down the grab button. You can drag players around after you grab them. This is useful for Team events where you need to keep other players away from something. You can also use it to mess with players who are trying to complete goals. Use it to push them in front of obstacles or mess up their timing. Be careful, though. Grabbing can easily backfire. If a player grabs you, move around and press the jump button to try and break out of it. If you see the grab coming ahead of time, you can also use your dodge move to get out of the way.

No matter how good you get at *Fall Guys*, you're bound to take a few spills from time to time. Even the best players don't win every match they join. But that's all part of the fun with this unique game. Keep trying, and always remember that the real goal is simply to have a good time!

Glossary

chaos (KAY-ahs) a state of confusion and disorder

cosmetic (kahz-MEH-tik) relating to how something looks

currency (KUR-uhn-see) a system of money

developers (dih-VEL-uh-purz) people who make video games or other computer programs

interface (IN-tur-fays) a way of interacting with a video game or other computer program

logic (LAH-jik) careful, reasoned thinking

microtransaction (MYE-kroh-trans-ak-shuhn) something that can be purchased for a small amount of money within a video game or other computer program

port (PORT) create a new version of a video game or other computer program that runs on a different device

precise (preh-SYSE) accurate and exact

servers (SUR-vurs) computers that host online games or other internet services

taunt (TAWNT) playfully annoy an opponent in a game

Find Out More

BOOKS

Cunningham, Kevin. *Video Game Designer*. Ann Arbor, MI: Cherry Lake Publishing, 2016.

Loh-Hagan, Virginia. *Video Games*. Ann Arbor, MI: Cherry Lake Publishing, 2021.

Powell, Marie. *Asking Questions About Video Games*. Ann Arbor, MI: Cherry Lake Publishing, 2016.

WEBSITES

Fall Guys Ultimate Knockout
https://fallguys.com
Check out the official *Fall Guys* site for the latest updates on the game.

Fall Guys: Ultimate Knockout Wiki
https://fallguysultimateknockout.fandom.com
This fan-created site is packed with info about every detail of *Fall Guys*.

Index

About the Author

Josh Gregory is the author of more than 150 books for kids. He has written about everything from animals to technology to history. A graduate of the University of Missouri–Columbia, he currently lives in Chicago, Illinois.